# *Words* OF WISDOM

# Words of WISDOM

Those with wisdom will shine as
the brightness as the sky

Book
No. 2

## ROY MARTIN

*Words of Wisdom*

Copyright © 2020 by Roy Martin. All rights reserved.

---

No part of this publication may be reproduced, stored in a retrieval system or transmitted in any way by any means, electronic, mechanical, photocopy, recording or otherwise without the prior permission of the author except as provided by USA copyright law.

The opinions expressed by the author are not necessarily those of URLink Print and Media.

---

1603 Capitol Ave., Suite 310 Cheyenne, Wyoming USA 82001
1-888-980-6523 | admin@urlinkpublishing.com

URLink Print and Media is committed to excellence in the publishing industry.

Book design copyright © 2020 by URLink Print and Media. All rights reserved.

---

Published in the United States of America

Library of Congress Control Number: 2020907532
ISBN 978-1-64753-331-1 (Paperback)
ISBN 978-1-64753-332-8 (Digital)

13.10.20

# Introduction

The scripture references are from the King James Version of the bible, with corrections of spelling of Old English words.

The words of wisdom for this book came from various sources; some from the bible, some from the authors personal experiences, some from "Old" sayings that contain a lot of wisdom, and some from insights to the author directly from God.

The words of wisdom in this book are in no particular order, so there are no chapters.

The author suggests that, if possible, you take this book with you so you can read it when you have to wait at the doctor's office, while riding a bus, etc. You may feel inclined to read it more than once.

Obviously, this is not an exhaustive study concerning wisdom. You can do your own research concerning wisdom, and make an appeal to God to provide you with wisdom.

It is understandable that some will disagree with what has been written in this book. The author respects your right to disagree.

# 1

As noted in Book No. 1, wisdom is still the
principle thing, so get wisdom. But in your
getting, get also understanding. (Proverbs 4:7)

Where can wisdom be found, and where is the place
of understanding? Wisdom cannot be purchased
with gold, or jewels, or pearls. To be fearful of God
is wisdom, and to depart from evil is understanding.
(Job 28:12-28)

> If your mouth speaks words of wisdom
> from the bible, the meditations of your
> heart will reveal understanding.
> (Psalms 49:3)

We cannot always do what we want to do. We must
do whatever is the most honorable thing to do.

If you would spend as much time developing
your heart as you spend developing your face,
people would enjoy your company more.

The world might owe you something, but
it will be a debt difficult to collect.

Deceivers are also subject to being deceived, and
probably don't realize it. (2 Timothy 3:13)

When dealing with people, expect
the unexpected to happen.

God did not tell us to love our neighbor instead of
ourselves.  He said to love our neighbor as much as
we love ourselves.  If we don't love ourselves, we will
not know how to love our neighbor. (Luke 10:27)

A deceived Christian is someone who has a form of
godliness, but denies or neglects the power of God.
(2 Timothy 3:5)

Pride will provide us with a mental rush,
but it is only temporary.  Pride will never
provide us with a sense of fulfillment.

Only as we forgive others and become
established in God's word can we be healed
of verbal, physical and emotional abuse.

We not only need to forgive those who have
wronged us, we must be quick to forgive. The
longer we delay forgiving the harder it becomes.

When the world's problems plague you,
lean into Jesus. You lean into him by
leaning into his teachings in the bible.

When you have love in your heart and
peace in your mind, any place is home.

Who you are does not influence your emotions
as much as who you believe your are.

Judging a person's actions is not the same as judging
their motives for their actions, which can lead to strife.

Faith is picturing in your mind
something done before it is done.

Faith in God is believing a kite can fly when there is
no wind if God tells you to fly a kite. (Genesis 18:14)

People demonstrate in the streets demanding their "rights". Why don't people demonstrate demanding their "responsibilities"? How can people have rights without responsibilities?

People feel more comfortable with Jesus' cross than they do with Jesus. Could it be because the cross doesn't talk back.

The key to receiving a benefit from God's glory is in your tongue, your words.
(Psalms 16:8-9; Acts 2:25-27)

Like a bird over the ocean, a curse without a cause (legal right) has no place to land. (Proverbs 26:2)

We don't know what the future holds, but we know who holds the future if God is true to his word.

Telling people about God's grace does not give people an excuse to sin. When you have experienced God's grace, you don't look for ways to sin and get away with it, you look for ways to keep from sinning.

To test a person's loyalty to his country, raise his country's flag and watch how the person reacts.

When you read the bible, you will experience either joy or offense. Joy if you are willing to do what it says, or offense if you are not willing to do what it says.

Loving others is just as important for a balanced life as being loved.

People who love only themselves are in a mental prison.

A crumb from God will bring you more joy than a whole loaf from Satan. (Mark 7:24-30)

God can not only save you from the fires of hell, he can save you from yourself, from selfishness.

Don't put your hope in yourself, in your abilities. Put your hope in the true God. Get grounded in the bible. It is a book of hope. (Romans 8:24-25)

People's criticism toward you will test your maturity.

Life begins to get complicated when we get around 18 years of age. We begin to think that soft drinks are too soft and God is too old fashion.

God knows we are not perfect in our conduct, but he still expects us to trust him.

Having a dear friend is like having money in
the bank.  You don't have to see the money, just
knowing it is there gives you a nice, warm feeling.

Speak your faith in God, not your fears.  To speak faith
you will need God's words in your heart in abundance.
(Matthew 12:34)

Hope that is not based on God's wisdom is false hope.
False hope is not actually hope, it is wishing.  True
hope has an intimate relationship with the true God.

Without faith in the true God, hope has no substance,
nothing solid to stand on, no place to land.

Relationships require at least two, so
you can't have a relationship with God
unless God is present in your life.

The man in the bible called John the Baptist
must have done something unique in the way he
baptized, that is why he was named after it.

Don't focus on things that cannot hurt you, such
as previous hurts.  They cannot continue to hurt
you unless you continue to focus on them.

Some people's promise to you is like the wind. It blows, and that is about all you can say about it.

Our first personal experience with God's Spirit is like eating one peanut, you suddenly hunger for more.

People cannot oppress your egotism
if you don't have any.

Love that is based solely on feelings will
be fragile, because feelings are fragile,

People who live in a glass house should not
throw stones. People whose feelings are
easily hurt should not hurt others.

The only difference between knowledge
and skill is practice. The only difference
between skill and mastery is time.

We cannot build our identity with God. We
can only receive our identity from God.

Love usually does not think with its head, it thinks with its heart. This is why its heart is easily broken.

Lust does not think with its head, it thinks with
is feelings. This is why lust is easily offended.

Hope is a good thing if it is based on the wisdom of the God who made heaven and earth. (Romans 15:13)

There is no substitute for forgiveness, not even goods or good works can substitute for forgiveness.

There is a word that lives. We find it by reading the written words in the bible concerning Jesus' earthly ministry. (John 1:14)

Our faith in God defies fate, because God defies fate. That was the heartbeat of the church when it first started. (Acts 16:5)

It would be wise to try to please God rather than trying to please yourself. Our faith in God pleases him the most. (Hebrews 11:6)

We acquire faith in God by reading what is recorded in the bible concerning what Jesus taught during his earthly ministry. You don't need to read the entire bible. Buy a bible that has Jesus' teachings printed in red letters, and read the red. (Romans 10:17)

A wise man said,"Live everyday as if it will be your last day on earth, because some day it will be."

We usually don't think of good advice or good counsel as coming from the spiritual world. The spirit of counsel is one of the seven spirits that God gave Jesus to function in this physical world. (Isaiah 11:2)

If you are old, don't think of yourself as a senior citizen, think of yourself as a citizen with seniority.

Serving God is a full time job. Don't sign up for that job unless you are willing to serve God full time.

Loving the way God wants us to love involves spiritual warfare, because we have a spiritual adversary that wars against us when we love the way God loves. That love exposes the adversary as a phony.

Your beauty can become your downfall if you misuse it or abuse it or depend upon it for a sense of fulfillment.

Be forewarned that your thinking might be too shallow. It could cause your relationships with others to be shallow.

Anything that is worth doing is worth doing right.

Man has the option to say to God, "Your will be done" or he can say, "My will be done."

Being thankful for what God has done for us is one way to worship God and express our love toward him. (Romans 5:8)

The days of powder puff Christianity need to come to an end and be replaced with boldness. But it is difficult to be bold without being filled with God's Spirit. (Ephesians 3:11-12)

God is a wise God. He knows how to use imperfect people to carry out his perfect will. (Matthew 16:18,23)

How do you tell a true God from a false God? A true God draws people to himself because of his goodness. (Romans 2:4)

He never gives people authority to rule over other people. He tells his servants to serve. (Matthew 20:27)

He allows people to make personal choices without threatening them. (Joshua 24:15)

However, he does warn those who make wrong choices. (Deuteronomy 11:26-28)

We should not only be thankful, but practice being thankful by telling those for whom we are thankful.

> Practicing being thankful will move us closer to the miraculous, closer to receiving and performing miracles.
> (Romans 1:21)

Defining people can be risky, but a "liberal" seems to be a person who believes there is such a thing as a free lunch, a lunch that no one has to pay for. The lunch will fall out of the sky.

Hell will seem like two eternities, because when you are in pain every hour seems like two hours.

Don't break the heart of the God that loves you.

Some people believe a balanced meal is when you have a cheeseburger in each hand.

When a boy meets a girl that he adores, he hopes he is her first love. The girl hopes she is his last love.

As long as you are just talking about your faith the Devil is winning. If you demonstrate your faith, the Devil is losing.

In your mind you may believe the God of love is the God that allows you to do whatever pleases you.

Sorrows that are not committed to God may fester into grievous sores.

Give the Devil an inch, and he will take a foot. Give the Devil your mind, and he will take your heart.

Your boldness in the face of an assault by a demon is proof to the demon that you have God on your side. You have God on your side when you have his word in your heart in abundance.

Pride is very bossy.

Depend on the peace of God to inform you if what you say or do pleases him. Allow God's peace to be the umpire in all you say and do.

Pride will cause you to have an unruly mouth.

Let the words of wisdom from God dwell in you richly. (Colossians 3:16)

Fathers, discipline your children, but don't provoke your children to the point that you cause them to become discouraged.

## 2

There is a big difference from being a
follower of Jesus and being a willing servant
of Jesus. A puppy dog can be a follower.

It is not a coincidence that the bible compares our
serving God to a Marathon runner. (Hebrews 12:1)

God's word is food for our faith. (Romans 10:17)

Love is not just something you show, you are
love. The physical act of love is just the end result
of being the embodiment of love. Without the
embodiment, love can only be a superficial love,
which is a form of love but not true love. The
bible says God is love. The bible says we are made
in God's image. (1 John 4:8; Genesis 1:27)

There is a time and a place for everything. When you see someone approaching the edge of a cliff, don't shout, "God loves you." Shout, "Stop."

> Wisdom will cause you to see
> through a lie as if it was glass.

Wisdom will show us whether or not the misery we are going through is self inflicted.

We are free to make choices, but we are not free to determine the consequences of our choices.

> If Jesus is not in your mouth, he is not
> in your heart, for out of the abundance
> of the heart the mouth speaks.
> (Matthew 12:34)

The truth you can bend is not really the truth.

> God does not always call those who are
> qualified. Rather, he will qualify those he
> calls to carry out his great commission.

> The most difficult musical instrument
> to play is second violin. There are many
> who believe they can play first violin.

Some people will use your self pity to blackmail you. This is why they will first condemn you.

It does not do any good to close the barn door after the horse has already run away. Instead, learn from your mistake and don't leave the door open next time.

If you do not relish praise, you will not be devastated by criticism.

When you discipline your children, remember there is a difference between a whipping and a beating.

How do you know you have fulfilled your mission in life? It is when you experience dying as though you are falling asleep. (Acts 7:60)

You can never be truly free unless you know the truth. God's word is truth. (John 8:32; 17:17)

If you want to find favor with God, ask him what is on his heart. Make it your goal to know God's heart.

If you do not love God as an act of your will, you will never experience God's kind of love, which exceeds willful love. (1 John 4:8-10)

Some people are somewhat like dogs. Feed them and they will stay with you. (John 6:26)

When a bear attacks us, I don't have to outrun the bear; I just have to outrun you.

The best time to have planted a tree was thirty years ago. The second best time is now.

If you fear death, whoever holds the threat of death over your head will be your master.

In creating the world, God did not rest on the seventh day because he was tired. He rested because he finished what he planned to do. God works, but he never gets tired. (Psalms 121:4)

Faith in God is the currency of the kingdom of God.

You have only one life to live, don't waste it.

If you are your own man, then you are not God's man.

Whoever has your ear has your future.

Preachers, preach with love, or else your words will be nothing but noise in the kingdom of God. (Ephesians 4:15)

The kingdom of God is not for sissies. (John 15:20)

Those involved in religion are determined to worship God according to their flesh, not according to their spirit. Our flesh is made out of dirt, dirt cannot worship God. The communion of bread and wine is not for worship, it for remembering who it is that we are to worship. (1 Corinthians 11:24-25)

> Most people want to know the truth, but not the truth about themselves.

Exalt wisdom, and wisdom will exalt you. Embrace wisdom, and wisdom will bring you honor. If you walk with wisdom, you will not stumble. (Proverbs 4:8)

> Become addicted to God. Daily contact for daily provisions.

God's hand is not so short that he cannot save, or his ear so deaf that he cannot hear. (Isaiah 59:1)

Don't be like the horse or the mule, who must be held in check with a bit and a bridle. Bridle your tongue yourself by an act of your will. (Psalms 32:9)

You may be just one instruction away
from your breakthrough.

A man never stands so straight as
when he stoops to help a child.

Husbands, be thankful if your wife has a heart
of gold, even though she may have a short fuse.
The heart of gold will offset the short fuse.

Are these words of wisdom: Do you love someone
because they are beautiful, or are they beautiful because
you love them? Is beauty in the eyes of the beholder?

God loves the vows that people make which
are in accordance to what we read in the bible.
Honoring our vows is sometimes referred to in
the bible as "paying" our vows. This is probably
what it will feel like when we fulfill our vows.

If faith was a race horse, trust would be his legs.
Trust is what carries him to his destination.

A riddle with wisdom: Those in bondage to God are
free. Where the Spirit of the Lord is there is liberty.
(2 Corinthians 3:17)

A thought to ponder: Were you raised
up, or were you jerked up?

God framed the world by words. We are made in
God's image. Does that mean we can frame our
world if we use God's words? (Proverbs 18:21)

Church leaders would be wise not to
confuse pomp with power. (Acts 4:33)

God's Spirit guides. (John 16:13) Satan's
spirit drives. (Luke 8:29)

Sometimes the hardest people to love
are those of your own household.

In order to make a dream come true, the
first thing you have to do is wake up. This
also applies to dreams for our life.

A change of your mind is dependent upon a change
of your heart if it is to become permanent.

Who you honor will have an impact on you,
whether you ever meet them in person or not.

Chocolate covered religion is just as
addictive as chocolate covered food.

> Do you say what you believe, or do
> you believe what you say?

Miracles have a voice. They speak to those who see the miracles. Some people choose to disagree with that voice. Some want to agree, but first want an explanation of how it happened. (Exodus 4:8) If you can explain a miracle, it would not be a miracle.

> If we commit ourselves to work for God,
> he will be with our mouth and tell it
> what to speak. (Exodus 4:12)

Woe unto those who call evil good and good evil. Woe unto those who are wise in their own eyes, and despise the word of God. (Isaiah 5:20-24)

To God's servants, God says, "I will contend with those who contend with you." (Isaiah 49:25)

Be slow to speak and quick to listen. (James 1:19)

> A riddle with wisdom: When is an animal
> not an animal? When it is a pet.

Being lazy will cause you to be irresponsible.

It is better to have one handful with quietness than two handfuls with strife. God hates strife. (Proverbs 6:16-19)

A fool will tell more than he knows.

If your word is good, your name is good. Could this be the reason that God elevated his word above his name? (Psalms 138:2)

You cannot change your heart for the better until you change your mind for the better.

Commit yourself to love what God loves, and hate what God hates.

Everyone is devoted to something or someone or some cause. God wired us to be that way. Your destiny will be in accordance to who or what you are devoted to.

Is your god your belly? If it is, you would be wise to admit it, at least to yourself. It might cause you to make some changes that will lengthen your life and lay claim to the abundant life that Jesus promised. (John 10:10)

In lifting up others, you lift up yourself.

Could you, in all honesty, say, "I am
a friend of God?" (James 2:23)

You can learn from your past, but you cannot
change it. So, don't waste your time rehearsing
in your mind the "what if" game.

A stronghold in your life is anything that has a
strong hold on you, whether good or bad.

Speak to yourself what God promised,
or else Satan will speak to you that God
is the cause of your problems.

Ask God to light your candle, then you will
walk in (spiritual) light. (Psalms 18:28)

With God's help we can run through a troop
and jump over a wall. (Psalms 18:29)

Your soul will never be at rest until it
finds rest in the one who made it.

If you have a voice, you have a choice;
a choice of what to speak.

A visitation from God is wonderful,
but an habitation is even better.

Words are like seeds. What you sow (speak) will produce after its own kind. You can't sow strife and expect to reap peace.

My future is not in bondage to my past, unless I allow it to be.

Don't trade the truth for a lie. If you do, you will trade God's word, which is truth, for a lie and worship what God created rather than God himself. (Romans 1:22-32)

The most misunderstood and misused word in the English language is probably the word "love". There are many types of love. There is a type of love that is not based on feelings, it is based on a vow or willful commitment. This why Jesus could command his followers to love one another. (John 15:17)

As a man thinks in his heart, so is he. (Proverbs 23:7)

God's words in the bible have the power to reveal you to you. Satan's words have the power to hide you from you.

Information without revelation has the potential to result in imitation. This is what happens when you have religion without wisdom. This allows Satan to become a god with many faces and many names.

Don't be filled with spirits (alcohol) that come from a bottle, but be filled with the spirit (Holy Spirit) that comes from God.

Being God's servant will be the best job you ever have.

Prayer to God has the power to give you wisdom. (James 1:5)

Do you just eat dessert or do you make love to it? This is how you will know if you are addicted to sugar.

The ideal job is to be a mortician. It is easy to cover up your mistakes.

God's words have the power to cause us to believe them if we speak them. This may be the reason some people avoid reading the bible. It convicts them of their sins. It would be an act of wisdom to read the bible even if it makes us uncomfortable.

If you don't hate evil, you probably won't fear God.

It is better not to make a vow than to make one and not honor your vow.

You are truly blessed if your
inheritance includes wisdom.

Wisdom is a covering, and money is a covering.
But wisdom can take you further in life than
money can, and will add no sorrow to it.

Spending time in God's word is the same as
spending time with God; which, in turn, is like
spending time with eternity. (John 1:1,14)

Our goal in life should be to progress to the
point where God's words sound like a trumpet
calling us into combat, to do battle with
Satan and his demonic angels that are trying
to influence people, including ourselves.

Praising God because of who he is, is critical;
especially when you are going through your
midnight hour-midnight hour of sickness, financial
problems, relationships, etc. (Acts 16:25)

The proof of the pudding is in the eating. The
proof of wisdom is determined by the end results.

# 3

The fool says in his heart, "There is no God." The wise say in their hearts, "What are the consequences if the fool is wrong?"

If you believe in God, but believe he has let you down, talk to him about it. (Psalms 13:1-6) He has ears that hear.

Be transparent before God, not for his benefit but for your benefit. Say in your heart, "I decree and declare that I will be transparent before God."

Hell is like a nightmare that you never wake up from, so there is no end.

It might be easier to love God if we knew that he loved us first. (1 John 4:19)

If you refuse the counsel of God and the counsel of God's servants, the only way you will learn the hard stuff is through suffering. Pain and fear will be your teachers, your counselors.

As a bridegroom rejoices over his bride, so shall God rejoice over you if you have acknowledged God as your God. (Isaiah 62:5)

Those with the wisdom of God will say in their hearts, "I shall arise and shine for the glory of God has risen upon me." (Isaiah 60:1)

When the cook of the family goes on a weight loss diet, everyone in the family loses weight. Words of wisdom can be humorous as well as helpful.

Only with the power of our anointing from God can we remove Satan's yoke from off our necks. (Isaiah 10:27)

Our failures may not be a bad thing if we learn something from them.

Before you start building anything, including a relationship with God, it would be wise to first sit down and count the cost. (Luke 14:28,33)

It may not sound like wisdom, but the best way you can overcome selfishness is to constantly look for things you can be thankful for. This would include the people in your life that you can be thankful for.

The voice of wisdom says, "Whatever God values, you must also value."

God will honor your obedience to him, but you may not realize what you are experiencing is coming from him, such as peace.

It doesn't do any good to bless people with your spoken words, then curse them under your breath.

Pride is a pit that even the wise might fall into.

Your voice of praise toward God sounds like music to God, the chief musician. (Habakkuk 3:1,19)

God should forever be your king, because you will forever be his beloved. (Ephesians 1:6; Romans 1:7)

We don't have to suffer in quiet desperation. We have an advocate who is our attorney. His name is Jesus. (Romans 8:34)

Husbands, you have a considerable amount of your
life invested in your wife. As a minimum, you should
consider her as one of your valuable investments.

In order to be more like Jesus and experience
God's love, we must fellowship with the
Holy Spirit. (2 Corinthians 13:14)

If you refuse God's discipline, how can you
claim his promises? (Psalms 50:16-17)

To continue to be wise, we must
continue to be teachable.

A wise person is willing to listen to many counselors,
even if he eventually rejects some of their advice
as not being appropriate for his situation.

Just because you don't believe something
does not mean it is false. For years people
did not believe the earth was round.

To command others, you must first learn to accept
commands from others, from those that are above you.

A chain is only as strong as its weakest link. This
is why every link needs to be examined. So

it is with our physical life and our spiritual life. Every link must be examined.

Satan wants your tongue. Don't let him have it. If he already has it, rebuke him in Jesus' name, and tell him you are taking your tongue back.

Without God's Spirit as our guide, we will never know God. So invite God's Spirit into your life.

The greatest joy we can experience is when we are in the Kingdom of God. The Kingdom of God is the first thing Jesus preached when he began his earthly ministry. (Matthew 4:17)

Preachers, if you are not preaching the Kingdom of God, you are not preaching the gospel, because the gospel is the gospel of the kingdom. (Matthew 4:23)

We should think as highly of ourselves as God does, but not any more than that. (Romans 12:3)

Our goal should be to be influenced more by God than by people, including ourselves.

Don't doubt God's promises. Rather, doubt your doubts about his promises.

Who told you that? Who told you that
everybody has to die due to bodily ailments,
that there is no such thing as a "natural" death?
We will die when we have completed our
mission in life, whether we are sick or not.
(Deuteronomy 34:7)

The law of the Old Testament demands righteousness.
Grace in the New Testament supplies righteousness.

Those with wisdom are like vintage
wine. They get better with age.

If you are God's servant, nothing shall by any
means hurt you, not even death. Death will be
like going to sleep. (Luke 10:19; Acts 7:59-60)

Those with wisdom will be swift to hear
and slow to speak. (Psalms 23:5)

God will fill the cup of the wise until
it overflows. (Psalms 23:5)

If Jesus does not want to have an intimate relationship
with the church, why does the bible refer to the
church as Jesus' bride? (Revelation 21:9)

Feel free to question God. He would
rather you question him than to mummer
against him. (Deuteronomy 1:27)

Would it be an act of wisdom if we spent
as much time reading the bible as we
spend socializing on our cell phones?

How can we miss what we have never known?
People don't miss having a relationship with God
because they have never known him. People don't
have a sense a fulfillment and don't know why.

We must also learn from other people's
mistakes, because we won't live long enough
to make all the mistakes ourselves.

To have a relationship with God, you not only have to
believe in God, you must know that he believes in you.

What you think in your heart is what
you are. (Proverbs 23:7)

There are times when we need to color within
the lines. There are times when we need to
create our own lines in which to color.

We need to have faith for the supernatural if
we expect to have supernatural results.

The Kingdom of God can be compared to a valuable
treasure, so valuable that we will gladly give everything
we own for that treasure. (Matthew 13:44)

Church, be aware of the signs of the last
days. One of those signs is the church will
have a form of godliness, but will neglect or
deny God's power. (2 Timothy 3:1-5)

Jesus did not come to the earth to show his followers
how to form a religion. He came to show his followers
how to have an abundant life. (John 10:10)

When you are alone, read the bible out loud
and notice if it impacts you differently than
when you read it under your breath.

We do not display God's glory in the
ornaments we wear or in the church
buildings we build. (Luke 21:5-6)

We demonstrate God's glory when his followers
use Jesus' name to heal the sick, cast out
demons, and raise the dead. (John 14:3)

God told the Israelites to eat unleavened bread at Passover because he did not want their appetites to enjoy the bread. The purpose was to subdue their bodies, so God could elevate their spirits. This is also the purpose for fasting.

It is not sufficient just to have knowledge of church history and Jesus' earthly ministry. We must have a personal relationship with God by inviting God's Spirit to come and dwell in us. (Luke 11:13)

Depend on God by serving him. He will light your candle so you will have light for your life. (Psalms 18:28)

Of all the well-known religions, Jesus is the only holy man whose name is sometimes used as a cuss word. This is not a coincidence. (Luke 23:35)

If you are your own man, then you are not God's man.

God is good to those that are wise enough to get bound up together with him. (Lamentations 3:25)

It would be wise to be as concerned about the interior of your body as you are about the exterior.

Our goal should be to progress to the point in
our relationship with God that we can stand
before him naked, like Adam and Eve did,
and not be embarrassed. (Genesis 2:25)

It is not a coincidence that the bible refers to
God as "The Father of lights." (James 1:17) This
is not referring to the light from the sun.

A riddle will sometimes contain wisdom:
Whoever desires to be great will be great if they
become a servant of all. (Matthew 20:26)

We will never know how to view God until
we know how he views us.(John 3:16)

Some people who act superior actually feel inferior.

Time does not wait for anyone, so use
wisdom in planning your day.

How can God be pleased if you love praises from
people more than praises from God. (John 12:43)

To help you stay humble, tell about the
stupid things you have done.

There is nothing wrong in being bossy as long as you are kind and considerate, and do your share of the work. Somebody has to be the boss.

Some people compare chaos as being like a bull in a china shop. Have you ever felt like your problems are the bull, and you are the china shop?

Like being saved from hell, forgiving hurts is not a head issue but a heart issue. (Matthew 18:35; Romans 10:9)

Your attitude is important to God. Your attitude will determine your altitude, how high you can go in the Kingdom of God. (Philippians 3:14)

People who gain in their finances in spite of competition never complain about the competition.

Stay hidden in Christ; then when trouble comes, it will not be able to find you. (Colossians 3:3)

You don't have to win the race to be a winner in God's eyes. Just be obedient to be a winner. Noah preached for 120 years, and never won a single convert, but he still found favor in God's eyes.

There is a risk involved in loving others. You risk being demoralized if they don't accept your love.

The more you know about God, the more you will know about yourself. You are made in his image and likeness.

Many people yearn to know God's will. God's word is God's will, so read the bible.

Lust can masquerade as love.

Your flesh is just as much the enemy of your soul as Satan. (Ephesians 2:3)

Be forewarned, Satan is an expert in tempting people.

Experiencing severe hardships will cause you to become better or bitter. Which one is your choice.

The joy of receiving God's Spirit in your life is like winning the lottery, but the benefits last longer in receiving God's Spirit. They last for eternity.

Rejoice if a perverted world persecutes you because you are obeying Jesus. A perverted world also persecuted Jesus. (John 15:20)

There is wisdom in that old song that says, "Sometimes our heart is a desert, and music is the rain."

God did not give us a spirit of fear; but of power, of love, and of a sound mind. (2 Timothy 1:7)

God's presence in our life brings rest. (Exodus 33:14)

When you pray to God, believe he hears you. (1 John 5:14)

We should not only have faith in what God says, but also have faith in what we say if we say it in accordance to what God says. (Mark 11:23)

God honors those who honor him.

Since the bible says love of money is the root of all evil, we can be tempted to do evil to get money whether we are rich or poor.

Don't let your sins make you too ashamed to read the bible. This is one of Satan's favorite tricks.

Loving someone who doesn't deserve to be loved is when love shows its greatest power. Husbands and wives, memorize this statement.

Believing is the first step to acquiring faith.

There are times when you need to be tough on yourself in order to make yourself do something you need to do, but do not want to do it.

# 4

Give instructions to a wise man and he will
become even wiser. (Proverbs 9:9)

Good instructions come from the bible. Read it daily.
You will draw from it instructions and strength.

The sinners wealth is his glory. (Isaiah 61:6)

The wealth of the sinner is laid up for those whose
heart is right before God. (Proverbs 13:22)

It is shameful to even speak of those things
that are done in secret. (Ephesians 5:12)

Those involved in secret societies, such as Free
Masonry, should heed this. If what is done is

wonderful, you should shout it from the house tops so everyone can enjoy it. (Luke 12:3)

Don't be surprised if a fool despises the wisdom of your words. (Proverbs 23:9)

Bodily exercise is profitable to the body, but godliness is profitable to all things. (1 Timothy 4:8)

It is not a coincidence that alcoholic beverages are referred to as "spirits". When you are under their influence, you connect with the dark spiritual world; and you come under its influence.

It requires supernatural power to forgive those that are in the process of killing you. (Luke 23:33-44)

God's type of godliness is revealed in his power, so we will not be able to claim that godliness if we depend solely on man's power.

The world is waiting for a manifestation of God's power from the church. Is the world just mostly seeing powerless religion? (Romans 8:19)

The shortest route to a person's heart is through their stomach. This is why with tasty food, you can capture a person's heart.

To turn from your sins is when you
acquire understanding. (Job 28:28)

When you try to turn from your sins and find out
how difficult it is, you are more understanding of
others who are trying to turn from their sin.

We have to learn to take the bitter with
the sweet. That is just the way life is.

Precious in the sight of God is the death
of his saints. (Psalms 116:15)

But their death is not a hurtful
experience. (Luke 10:19)

Death is like going to sleep. (Acts 7:60)

If you want to know what your passion is, notice
what drives you. Does hate drive you?

You were not born in a box, so feel free to think
outside of the box that other people try to put you in.

When you are running life's race, keep your
eyes on the prize. (Philippians 3:4)

Continue to lift up God's word. It will
help build up your faith muscle.

It would be wise to continue to read the bible
daily. It will keep you on the right path.

Think of your life as a journey. Plan as you would
plan for a long journey; what you will do at a young
age, middle age, old age, death and after death.

In order to be a good leader in God's kingdom, we
first have to be a good follower in God's kingdom.

For some people, sugar and sugar substitutes
are just as addictive as cocaine. You
would be wise to remember that.

Do not speak into the ears of a fool, for he will
despise the wisdom of your words. (Proverbs 23:9)

Give God your best, then expect to receive his
best, his peace. (Haggai 2:8-9; Luke 2:13-14)

Don't be overly concerned about fighting the giants
in your life if God is with you like he was with David
in the bible. David's fight with Goliath would not
have glorified God if Goliath had been a midget.

How can God reject you if he is embracing you?

When you forgive others, don't keep a record of the number of times you have forgiven them. If you do you will miss the joy you are entitled to because you have forgiven them.

If you want to teach someone something, the first thing you have to do is get their attention. In the Old Testament God said he would put dung on the face of those who offered for a sacrifice animals with a blemish. That will get their attention. (Malachi 2:3)

If you control a horse's mouth, you can control his body. If you control your mouth, you can control your body. (James 3:3)

There is wisdom in some of the old church hymns, especially the one that says, "Trust and obey, for there is no other way to be happy in Jesus, but to trust and obey."

Don't speed read the bible. Read it slowly, prayerfully and frequently. That would be an act of wisdom.

It is time for Christians to come out of their closets. Everybody else is coming out of their closets. If Christians don't come out, they will get left behind.

If we truly worship God, why do we have
to go to the world to find our joy or fun?
We will find our joy casting out demons,
healing the sick and raising the dead.

When you are confident that you are doing God's work, take man's criticism as a compliment, and as proof that you are doing God's work. (Acts 5:41)

Wear your praises toward God as you would wear a royal garment before a king. (Psalms 22:3; 56:12)

Just because God gives you a dream, that does not mean you have to share it with everybody. Some people can't handle your dreams. (Genesis 37:5)

He that walks with the wise becomes
wise. (Proverbs 13:20)

Some people, because they have been hurt, hurt others.

If left untreated a heartache could end in a heart attack.

We might need to make praising God a ritual
in order not to forget to praise him. But a
ritual should never replace sincerity.

Where you focus your eyes can cause you a lot of trouble. Seeing can create a desire. For an example, if you know desserts are not good for your health, don't even look at them. Looking at the forbidden fruit in the Garden of Eden is what caused Eve to eat it. (Genesis 3:6)

You would be wise to choose God's peace toward you to be the umpire in deciding whether or not what you are planning to do pleases God. (John 14:27)

The idols and statues that people make may look like some person or some thing in its physical appearance, but their spirit is the spirit of the person who made them. This is man making a god in man's own image.

Faith in God is actually faith in his word. Faith in his word is actually faith in his integrity.

Where our own life is concerned, our words have more power than God's words. (Proverbs 6:2; Malachi 3:13)

This is why God's words must become our words if we expect to please God.

Young men, incline your ear to God's wisdom and instructions. The lips of an ungodly woman drip

with honey. Remove yourself from her. Don't
even go near her house. (Proverbs 5:1,3,8)

We cannot glorify God to the world until
God glorifies us. (John 17:22)

If God cannot free us from the fear of death, we can
never be truly free. (Romans 8:2; Hebrews 2:14-15)

Don't tell God how much you love him if you are not
willing to change and do what he says. (Psalms 55:19)

How we handle spiritual challenges will determine
how we handle natural challenges. (Luke 16:12)

You would be wiser than the majority of the people
in the world if you knew the significance of "little".
Multiply what you spend every day for a little item
times the number of days you expect to live, then
notice the final figure. Example: A pack of cigarettes
is a little item. If it cost $5.00, and you smoke a
pack a day, and you smoke for 50 years, your total
cost is $91,250.00. Calculate this for each little
item you consume daily, then add all of the totals
together to get a total for all of the "little" items you
consume. Do this calculation for each member of
your household, then add all of the totals together
to arrive at a grand total for the whole household.

God enjoys hearing his children speak his name. As you speak to God's heart, he will speak to your heart. (Jeremiah 33:3)

We honor people with our face, not our back. (Jeremiah 32:33)

If songs of praise to God go over and over in your head begging to be sung, sing them; even if you sing them under your breath.

Being involved in the public arena is not an option, it is an obligation for those living in a country with a democratic form of government. In a democratic government, if we don't use it we will lose it. A word to the wise should be sufficient to prompt action. (Proverbs 29:2)

It would be an act of wisdom if you would believe that the real "you" is a spirit that lives in a physical body, which will eventually cease to exist. Your spirit will continue to exist, but not on earth. It will be in heaven or hell.

The most powerful words that Jesus spoke during his earthly ministry were, "Follow me." He is still speaking those words to us through his Spirit. (Matthew 9:9)

Forbidden fruit always tastes good. If it didn't, we would not eat it, and it would not have to be labeled "forbidden". So, we can't use our taste to determine if something is forbidden. We must depend on God's word.

If you become like a child in the presence of God, he will become your security blanket. (Proverbs 18:10)

If you need advice concerning money, don't seek it from someone who could be wrong 100% of the time and never miss a pay check. Rather, seek advice from someone whose pay check is dependent upon him being right.

If we want to walk in the power of God, we must first walk in the compassion of Jesus. (Matthew 14:14)

It is better to trust God than to put your confidence in a person. (Psalm 118:8)

Cast your fears and anxieties over on God, then they become his property. He knows how to deal with them.
(1 Peter 5:7)

Decree and declare that you will not be stuck in the past, but will depend on the bible and God's voice to show you how to deal with your future.

If you want to please God, you would be wise not to take on a project that does not advance the Kingdom of God.

Speak your desires to God. He is just as interested in them as you are. He will use your desires to "connect" with you. (Psalms 37:4-5)

It is impossible to comprehend the love of God if we focus only on our fleshly body and the physical world. God is a spirit, and we connect with him through his words and our words. (John 6:63)

You may need to make some physical sacrifices in order to obtain spiritual fulfillment.

Being kind toward the poor will bring us a blessing from God. (Psalms 41:1)

Don't be anxious about tomorrow. Each day comes with its own troubles. (Matthew 6:34)

What appears to be impossibilities are not always based on facts. Sometimes they are just someone's opinion.

Our words reveal our spirit and our life. (John 6:63)

Don't be hard on yourself or others. Satan will do that.

> What is a spiritual sacrifice to God? It is being obedient when you don't feel like being obedient. (1 Peter 2:5)

What is the valley of decision that is mentioned in the bible? This is the place where we are trying to make a decision as to whether we will serve God or serve ourselves. (Joel 3:14)

It is more comfortable to study the historical Jesus than to study the "in your face" Jesus. (John 8:44)

If you have a bias concerning the bible, you will probably believe the bible agrees with your bias.

Don't expect your life to get better if you are not willing to make the changes that are necessary for your words to align with God's words.

It will help you to understand the New Testament of the bible better if you understand that the bible addresses three distinct groups of people: the Jews, the Christians, and the world (which is everybody else).

> We must be careful not to worship the
> works of our hands. (Jeremiah 1:16)

> If we chase after vanity, we will
> become vain. (Jeremiah 2:5)

> The same thing that breaks your heart
> also breaks god's heart if you are one of
> his children. (Luke 4:18; John 8:44)

Do not have fellowship with the unfruitful works of darkness, such as Halloween. (Ephesians 5:11) The fact that Halloween must be celebrated after dark should tell us all we need to know about Halloween.

# 5

People will know what God's love looks like when they see how his children respond to criticism and abuse. (Matthew 5:11-12; Acts 5:40-41)

Our faith should not be in man, but God. (1 Corinthians 2:4-5)

When the kingdom of heaven comes to earth, the supernatural becomes natural for those that embrace it. (Luke 10:9; John 6:5-11)

Wisdom from God is not just information, it is a spirit. (Isaiah 11:2; Ephesians 1:17)

You cannot discern a spiritually minded person if you are only physically minded. (1 Corinthians 2:14)

According to the bible, we have what we say.
So, several times a day, every day, say "I am
blessed. I am wise. I am in good health."
(Mark 11:23)

Some people that choose to be your enemies
you cannot defeat, but with wisdom and
forgiveness you can outlive them.

To go into God's throne room boldly, you have to
know your position with God. (Hebrews 4:14-16)

Our inheritance in the Kingdom of God is the same
as Jesus' inheritance if we accept God as our father.
That is why Jesus calls us his "brothers" and "sisters".

Anyone who condones what is harmful
to you is not your friend.

You can disarm some Christians with humor. While
laughing, they drop their guard. So, don't laugh at sin.

Your friends may forget you as time goes by, but
God will never forget you. (Isaiah 49:15-16)

When the Kingdom of God advances,
confrontation with the Kingdom of Darkness is
inevitable. (Luke 11:20; 2 Timothy 4:3-5)

It would be wise to be committed to the
truth, even if the truth hurts your pride.

Our stewardship from God is filled with warfare. Why,
because we have an adversary. His name is Satan.

It is good to draw near to God. Then he will
draw near to us. (Psalms 73:28; James 4:8)

How do we draw near to God? With our words. Our
words are us, and God's words are God. (John 1:1)

To walk in the peace of God, we must
first make peace with God.

You may not feel God's love when he says, " I love
you." But you will experience God's love when you say,
"God loves me." You have what you say. (Mark 11:23)

God's word can do whatever God can do,
because God's word is God. (John 1:1)

Go toward God, who is your father. When he sees
you coming, he will run to meet you. (Luke 15:20)

The past is past, so don't dwell on it
except to learn from your mistakes.

Your goal in life should be to get to
the point where you can talk to God as
friends talk to friends. (James 2:23)

Man cannot live by bread alone, because he is
spirit, which must have spiritual food. God's
words are spiritual food. (John 6:63)

We cannot measure God by our limitations.

You need to get ready for your next life by spending
time in God's word. Then when you get to heaven,
you won't feel like you are living among strangers.

Let your number one request from God be wisdom,
even for small things. Wisdom is the principle
thing, even among small things. (Proverbs 4:50)

You cannot make correct decisions without
correct information. This is why Satan
tries to distort your information.

For a wise man, his boundaries are inside
him, in his wisdom. For a fool, someone
else determines his boundaries.

Even if you have faith in God, you still need wisdom
because your circumstances will stretch your faith.

It is amazing how close we can be to
contentment and still miss it.

Hear and receive God's word, then the years
of your life will be many. (Proverbs 4:10)

A God kind of life is all about compassion.
Without compassion we become more like
animals, and live by our senses, our instincts.

In order for liberty to be permanent, it must
be balanced with responsibility. It would be
an act of wisdom if America built a Statue of
Responsibility on the west coast to balance
the Statue of Liberty on the east coast.

If we are not hungry and thirsty for the power of
God, we will not press forward and do what is
necessary to receive that power. (Matthew 5:6)

God's mercy is available to those who
show mercy toward others.

Whoever made time, made a lot of it, but your
portion of that time is very limited. So, try to make
every minute of your portion count for something.

If people knew how short life is, they would spend more time thinking about their next life, and prepare for it. It won't be here on the earth.

Be open if God asks you to explain to people about how to prepare for the next life.

When the righteous reign, the nation has a reason to rejoice. When the unrighteous reign, the nation mourns. (Proverbs 29:2)

Be swift to hear, to listen, but slow to speak or show wrath. (James 1:19)

Don't play games with eternity. Eternity is forever, and ever, and ever. etc.

Some people believe the bible has a long shelf life, so they let it sit on a shelf waiting for a convenient time to read it. The bible does have a long shelf life, but you don't.

If you do not overcome, you will be overcome. There is always someone who wants what you have. Even demons want your physical body, so they can function in the physical world.

You can be smart in book learning,
and still not be wise.

If you lock your doors at night, you don't
really believe in situational ethics.

Your spirit has to have your body to function in the world, the physical realm. When your body dies, your spirit has to leave the earth. Where it goes is due to the choices you make before your body dies.

Merely believing in the true God will not save
you. Satan believes in God. (James 2:19)

To be saved requires obedience.
(2 Corinthians 10:6)

God will honor those who honor him. (1 Samuel 2:30)

Is God's arm so short that he cannot save? (Isaiah 50:2)

Hear what God says to those that serve him, "The gold, silver and earth are mine, and I want to give them to you because you are mine". (Haggai 2:8)

Wives, if your husband calls you "Sugar", that means he is addicted to you or he is a master deceiver. You have to decide which one.

Changing your life by what you decree will
change your life by degrees, little by little.

You cannot embarrass someone who is mentally
retarded. You can give them a cussing, and
they will just stand there and smile back at you.
The next time someone gives you a cussing,
you would be wise to pretend to be mentally
retarded and just smile back at them.

We should set aside a quiet time to hear from God,
then he won't have to interrupt our day to talk to us.

God has promised to heal your broken heart
if you will trust him. (Psalms 147:3)

Money is a good servant, but a terrible master.

Having God's blessing does not mean you
can do as you please. (Malachi 2:1-2)

God wants us to be his beloved.
(Colossians 3:12; Romans 1:7)

If God cannot touch you with his
word, he cannot bless you.

Some people view God as their enemy. They believe God will hinder their enjoyment of life. If he does, he will replace it with a greater enjoyment that you can take to the grave with you.

Everyone who is proud in his heart is an abomination to God. (Proverbs 16:5)

It is shameful to make a decision concerning a problem before you have heard all the facts. (Proverbs 18:13)

Dealing with a fool and his folly is like dealing with a mother bear that has been robbed of her cubs. (Proverbs 17:12)

# 6

Any nation that tolerates lawlessness can
expect lawlessness to continue.

The beginning of strife is like the beginning
of a crack in the dam holding a large
body of water. (Proverbs 17:14)

Those who justify the wicked will
probably condemn the righteous.

A merry heart does good, like a good medicine.
A broken heart makes the bones feel dry.
(Proverbs 17:22)

Your prayers to God do not have to be eloquent,
but they must come from your heart.

Put it to a test. Read your bible for 30 minutes each day for 30 days, and see if it changes your life for the better. Start with the book of John in the New Testament portion of the bible.

God is a spirit, and his words are life. His words created life. We are also spirit, and our words are life if we say what God tells us to say. (John 6:63)

God will always be gracious toward us, but his grace will not benefit us if we refuse to receive it.

Jesus brings us peace. The world brings us trials and turmoil. (John 14:27)

God's word is faith food. It nourishes our spirit so we can run the race of life. (John 6:31-33)

Woe to those who strive with their maker. (Isaiah 45:9)

In order for us to have access to the power of God, we have to decree and declare the power of God. (Joshua 1:8)

Here is wisdom: When you are driving and approaching a green traffic light, don't ask yourself,

"If it turns red, can I make it in time?" Rather, ask yourself, "If it turns red, can I stop in time?"

When you are talking to God, has he ever put you on "Hold" while he attends to some other business?

Pride will open a door in our life that gives Satan a legal right to come through.

Pride will prompt us to depend on our own knowledge and strength to serve God rather than his words.

Satan hates with an intensity that is difficult for us to understand. All we need to understand is that his goal is to steal, kill and destroy. (John (10:10) But he will masquerade as an angel of light. (2 Corinthians 11:14)

In God's presence is fullness of joy. (Psalms 16:11)

We are in God presence when we read his word, because God's word is God. (John 1:1)

We not only have to hear God's words, but do what the words say. (James 1:22)

The bible condones the use of a paddle or switch to discipline unruly children. (2 Samuel 7:14) But we need to make a distinction between a whipping and a beating. (Ephesians 6:4)

If you get angry when someone interrupts you while you are talking, ask yourself, "Is it worth going to war over?"

God wants to have a personal relationship with you. God wants to give you the treasures of darkness. (Isaiah 45:3)

If you work yourself to death working for God without him commissioning you, your death will be a suicide, not a martyrdom. (Psalms (46:10)

You can see the level of a person's faith in God by his works. (Mark 2:1-5)

The true God loves people that don't deserve to be loved. (John 3:16-17)

Don't be surprised if God offends your mind in order to gain access to your heart. (John 6:48-51)

Jesus said, "Hear and do." (Matthew 7:24)

Jesus is to us "wisdom". (1 Corinthians 1:30)

It is difficult to get someone to believe the truth
if the truth adversely affects their salary.

Repeating the words of a liar makes us a liar,
even if our desire is to tell the truth.

How we perceive Jesus will determine
how we will approach him.

Warring with Satan can be very tiring. Refuse to
give up. Remember, you have the Power of Attorney
to use the name of Jesus. Use it on Satan.

The more we sacrifice for God, the
less it seems like a sacrifice.

Words of truth about yourself can hurt
your ears if it involves something you are
not willing to admit. (Acts 7:51,57)

Don't look for the living among the dead.
Memories can be very powerful. (Luke 24:1-8)

In God's kingdom, honor is dependent upon
honesty. Lying to yourself is the same as lying
to God and other people. (Proverbs 6:16-19)

Sometimes patience requires longsuffering.
Longsuffering is when you suffer a long time.
(1 Peter 3:20)

If God has assigned you a task to do, he will
go before you; so do not be discouraged
or fearful. (Deuteronomy 31:8)

Don't allow your pain to stop you from praising God;
rather, use your pain to remind you to praise God.

Rejoice that you don't have to be perfect in order
to qualify for God's love. (1 John 4:19)

If you will allow him, God will fill your
cup until it runs over. (Psalms 23:5)

We will either dominate Satan, or be dominated
by Satan. We can dominate when Jesus gives
us authority to use his name. (Mark 16:17)

When God becomes our head, we become
the head to the world; not the tail.
(Deuteronomy 28:13)

If the devil comes looking for you, he won't be able to find you if you are hid in Christ. (Colossians 3:3)

If your root is holy, you are holy. If your root is unholy, you are unholy. (Romans 11:16)

There can be wisdom in an allegory: A lazy man will sit a long time with his mouth open, hoping a roasted duck will fly in.

Those who roar like a bear will mourn like a dove if they neglect to prepare for Judgment Day. (Isaiah 59:11)

Your expectations will die with you, so make every stroke count while you are alive.

Be soft and pliable in the hands of God, and he will give you the desires of your heart. (Psalms 37:4)

We cannot use physical things to satisfy spiritual hunger. These two compete for your attention.

As the oceans are full of water, God's judgments are full of his righteousness. (Psalms 36:6)

Our God is great and infinite in
understanding.  (Psalms 147:5)

Our wisdom from God is a spirit, and it can be
transferred to others by our spoken word and
our written word.  (Deuteronomy 34:9)

Being a servant of God will make the
world's attractions less attractive.

When we read about Satan in the bible, it seems as
though he never sleeps and never takes a vacation.

To receive a blessing from God, stay as closely
connected to Jesus as a branch is to a tree.
(John 15:5)

Hear the wisdom from God:  Trust me with
your most private thoughts.  I will store them
on my secure web site.  No one will have the
password but me.  (Matthews 11:28-30)

Allow God to share his thoughts
with you.  (Jeremiah 29:11)

It is a historic fact that the impassioned few will
control the thinking of the neutral majority.  How

do you identify the impassioned few? It is the group with the loudest voice and the most persistence.

If you are guilty, don't pray for justice; pray for mercy.

Can a man rob God? God says his servants can by withholding the tithe, which belongs to God. (Malachi 3:8)

Your prayers to God have the power to give you wisdom. (James 1:5)

Don't put off until tomorrow what you can do today. Tomorrow will have its own problems.

You are not the captain of your own soul. Man has always had a boss, from the day he was created; either God or Satan, whichever we chose. If we don't choose God, we get Satan by default.

God hearing you call him Father brings him much pleasure, even though he knows you are not perfect in your conduct.

Wisdom is a treasure. (Colossians 2:3)

Be aware that people don't distract you from serving God by their humor and festivals. (Colossians 2:8)

Liberty without a feeling of responsibility
will end in reckless behavior.

What God has blessed no one can reverse,
so search for what God has blessed.

When we are in pain, a minute can seem like an hour.
When we are joyful, an hour can seem like a minute.

When someone's criticism of you is
justified, you would be wise not to ignore
it and not try to get revenge.

Hardships can make you better or
bitter, the choice is yours.

If you don't have a close relationship with
God, you will be bullied by fear.

Maintaining freedom is everybody's job.
Remember, your freedom ends where
other people's freedom begins.

If we want to walk in the power of Jesus, we
must first walk in the compassion of Jesus.
(Matthew 14:14)

Be wise concerning the devil's deception. If he can deceive you into believing his words toward you are actually your words, there is a strong possibility you will believe those words. Why? It is because you will believe you more than you will believe anybody else.

Some trust in things or someone to provide them with a sense of fulfillment, but these can only provide temporary pleasure. Only the true God can provide a sense of fulfillment. (Psalms 20:7-9; 145:19)

Focus your eyes on God's words, then you won't be blindsided. (Joshua 1:8)

Could God be sad because his followers are too pious to accept the sinner's wealth that God has laid up for them? (Proverbs 13:22)

Sometimes our posture reveals our attitude, our mind set.

Meet God's conditions, then you will meet God personally. If you have desires toward God, God will have desires toward you.

True love is the most powerful weapon on earth. Weapon? Yes, weapon. It is the only weapon that defeats hate, the most destructive weapon on earth. (1 Corinthians 13:8)

If we believe God, we will see his glory. God's glory is his goodness. (Exodus 33:18-19)

The day will come when the suffering will be so great that the living will envy the dead. (Ecclesiastes 4:1-2)

Satan is the father of lies. (John 8:44) Does that mean he is the spiritual father of liars?

# 7

The words of God can transform our life.  The more we learn God's words, the more of our life will be transformed.

Jesus was not born obedient to God.  He learned obedience by the things he suffered.  (Hebrews 5:8)  This is proof that sometimes something good can come from suffering.

We will probably not taste God's goodness until we learn to trust him.  (Psalms 34:8)

Faith in God will do for your spirit what vitamins will do for your body.

God's words are life. The more of his
words we have in us, the more of God's
life we will have in us. (John 6:63)

You would be wise to get serious about
your relationship with God.

A word of wisdom for preachers: Are you
spreading the gospel, or are you spreading
religion? They are not always the same.

Life is all about choices. Choose right now
who you will serve. To serve yourself is the
same as serving Satan, because he will take
advantage of you serving yourself.

God does not force his way into your life the
way Satan does. God comes into your life
only by invitation. (Revelation 3:20)

We have to be careful that we don't feel a closer kinship
with the animal kingdom than we do with God's
kingdom. How could God be pleased with that?

The quickest way to disarm a Christian is with
humor. Christians, be on guard and watch for this.

If you burn incense to a false god, you are
burning incense to vanity.  (Jeremiah 18:15)

You would be wise not to bring into your home
ornaments and figurines made by those who worship
false gods.  Those things are accursed, and you will
be adversely influenced by them.  They are usually
beautifully crafted.  (Deuteronomy 7:25-26)

Even lions will sometimes go hungry, but
those that put their trust in the true God will
not lack what they need.  (Psalms 34:10)

Your passion in life will drive you.  If it
doesn't drive you where you need to go,
you need to seek a new passion.

If God's back is his goodness, we can only
imagine what his face is.  (Exodus 33:18-23)

Those who go around in circles are called WHEELS.

We would be wise to press toward the mark
that qualifies us for the prize.  That mark is
servanthood toward God.  (Philippians 3:14)

It surely must grieve God if he has to
compete with food for your affections.

What God has blessed no one can
curse. (Numbers 23:20)

God gives his servants a tongue like the learned,
so they can speak a word of encouragement
to those that are weary. (Isaiah 50:4)

If your words are anointed by God, those that
hear you cannot ignore you. They will want
to hug you or hit you. (Acts 7:54-58)

In order for you to rule in God's kingdom, you
must first be willing to be ruled by God.

Every word you speak has consequences, but the
consequences may be delayed. This is why you may
never connect your words with the consequences.

Speaking words, even under your breath, establishes
them in your heart. When they get in your heart in
abundance, they will come out of your mouth out
loud, maybe when you least expect it. (Mark 12:34)

Anyone who will steal for you will steal from you.

God's words have a mind of their own. If you
memorize key scriptures, and rehearse them in

your mind daily, they will come up when you
need them, even without you calling them up.
(Joshua 1:8)

Your serving God will offend some people, so
expect to have to deal with them. Some of those
people might be in the church you attend, or in
your family. (Luke 12:52; Matthew 23:2)

You will be known by the company you keep,
those you choose to keep company with.
(1 Corinthians 5:9-11)

Love is not true love if it is never demonstrated,
such as an act of kindness or an act of giving.

Birds of prey never sing. People that prey
on others might find it difficult to sing,
even those that have the ability to sing.

The world loves worldly church
people. (John 15:19-20)

If you miss God's will when you give with a
sincere heart, you will not lose your reward.
(2 Corinthians 9:7)

God promised to keep us in perfect peace if we continually focus on him. (Isaiah 26:3) How do we focus on God, who is a spirit? We focus on his word, because God's word is God. (John 1:1)

We tend to become like whatever we focus on continually. (Philippians 4:8)

The most powerful force in the world is the true God. The second most powerful force in the world is the false god. Both of these can demonstrate their power through people. (Matthew 6:13; 9:8; Luke 4:6)

If your desire for perfection becomes an obsession, your desire for perfection may not be from God. It may be a demon trying to get back into God's favor by trying to be perfect.

A word of wisdom for church members: Don't call the church you attend "your" church. Call it Jesus' church. (Matthew 16:18)

It is required of stewards that they be found faithful stewards in whatever is entrusted to them. (1 Corinthians 4:2)

To be righteous in God's eyes, believe what God says.
Believe it strongly enough to act on it. (James 2:23)

Who defines who you are? Who decides how
much you are worth? If you do it, you will over
do it or under do it. Why not let God do it.

The bible uses pictures drawn by words to convey
its message. If we don't understand the picture,
we will not understand its message. God said he
was Israel's husband when they went a whoring
after other gods. What message does this convey?
(Jeremiah 31:32; Judges 2:17; Isaiah 54:5)

How do we distinguish love from
lust? Love gives. Lust takes.

Our life on earth can be compared to the
board game we call Monopoly. Even if we get
it all, in the end it all goes into the box.

According to the bible, we can ask God for wisdom
and expect to receive it if we ask in faith.
(James 1:5-6)

Pride and godly wisdom are not
compatible. (Proverbs 11:2)

According to the bible, pride is a wisdom killer. (Proverbs 6:16-19)

Think with your mind, not your feelings.

To put some fervor in your "soul winning", imagine that you are rescuing someone from a house that is on fire.

If you want to love your life and see good days, choose carefully the words you speak, including the words you speak to yourself. (1 Peter 3:10)

If you take a good look at your own behavior, you might start viewing other people differently.

Is God's arm so short that he cannot save? (Isaiah 50:2)

Although he was naked on the cross, Jesus was not ashamed because God was with him. (Isaiah 50:7)

Your battleground is your mind, not your flesh. Your body will go wherever your mind takes it. (Romans 12:2-3)

Blessed are those whose God is the
true God. (Psalms 144:15)

Blessed are those that find wisdom and
understanding. (Proverbs 3:13)

God, the true God, is our portion if we are his
servants. We can put our hope in him.
(Lamentations 3:24)

Hope that can be seen is not hope. We hope
for what we can discern without seeing it.
(Romans 8:24-25)

Fearing the true God is the beginning
of wisdom. (Psalms 111:10)

If your happiness depends on you receiving
praise, you live in a very small world.

The world is waiting for, and hoping for, a
manifestation, a demonstration of the power of
God from the servants of God. (Romans 8:19)

Husbands, love your wives as much as you
love yourselves. (Ephesians 5:25)

Choose your words carefully, so your words will not become a burden to you. (Jeremiah 23:36)

When you love, you become vulnerable. Love can be grieved. Love can be hurt.

Blessed is the nation whose God is the true God. (Psalms 33:12)

If you are God's servant, he will contend with those who contend with you. (Isaiah 49:25)

Whoever you fear the most will be the one you serve.

Sometimes we look, but we don't see. To actually see requires a determined focus. (2 Corinthians 4:18)

When we experience God's consuming fire, we will have the sensation of being hot without burning.

It is difficult for us to comprehend the influence that the invisible world has on the visible world.

For a democratic form of government to function, the majority of the people must have respect for those who disagree with them.

God inhabits the praises that his servants
have for him.  (Psalms 22:3)

God has promised that if we will serve him,
we will be the head and not the tail.
(Deuteronomy 28:13)

Revenge seems sweet at the beginning, but in the end
there is bitterness and sorrow and a lack of fulfillment.

The bible says those who win souls for
God are wise.  (Proverbs 11:30)

We don't want to be like those in the bible
who strain at a gnat and swallow a camel.
(Matthew 23:23-25)

What breaks your heart, also breaks God's
heart.  It is called compassion.

This does not sound logical, so it must be wisdom:
The best way to keep your joy is to share it with others.

Strife will negate your purpose
for fasting.  (Isaiah 58:4)

In order to soar above your problems, you have to learn how spread your wings. The bible will tell you how to spread your wings. Start with the book called JOHN.

> Some people who think they are praying to
> God are actually praying to themselves.
> (Luke 18:11-12)

> Trust is faith in action. This is
> the way to test your faith.

> Don't get offended if someone complains about
> you being a perfectionist. There are some situations
> where being a perfectionist is an asset.

> God is not far off in the distance.
> He is only a prayer away.

> It would be an act of wisdom on our part
> if we would not only seek peace but pursue
> it, chase after it, including peace within
> our own families. (Psalms 34:14)

> If you are one of his, God's blessings will chase
> you down the road and overtake you.
> (Deuteronomy 28:2)

What will you say when God corrects you? Try one of these: Yes, Sir. No, Sir. No excuse, Sir.

A house divided against itself cannot stand. (Mark 3:25) Sometimes the bible refers to a nation as a "house".

Unless God builds the house, those that build it labor in vain. (Psalms 127:1-2)

Could restful sleep be a gift from God? The bible has a lot to say about rest. (Matthew 11:28-30)

Could restful sleep at night increase our joy during the day? Joy can then increase our strength. (Nehemiah 8:10)

Jesus knocks on your door with his voice, so listen for his voice. (Revelation 3:20)

Our intimate relationship with God's Spirit is described in the bible as the "water of life" or "living water". (John 4:7-10)

He who exalts himself will eventually be humbled. He who humbles himself in God's presence will be exalted. (Matthew 23:12)

To be a son or daughter of the most high God, we must be willing to be led by God's Spirit. (Romans 8:4)

It would be an act of wisdom not to be proud of your humility.

He that is cruel, troubles his own flesh. (Proverbs 11:17)

# 8

Evil people don't understand justice. (Proverbs 28:5)

Wisdom is dependent upon knowledge. Know that Satan comes to steal, destroy and kill. Satan is a spirit. You can only fight him with spiritual weapons, Jesus words. (John 6:63)

God knows all about you; the good, the bad, the ugly. But he still loves you. He looks forward to you coming home to heaven. But the choice is yours. (John 3:16-21)

Don't be afraid of those who can kill you. Rather, be afraid of the one who can cast your soul into hell, to be tormented for eternity. (Matthew 10:28)

To be truly honorable requires us to
be humble. (Proverbs 15:33)

Not forgiving others will interfere with
our faith in God. (Matthew 6:15)

Worrying about your sin is a sin. You are not being
obedient. (1 Peter 5:7; 2 Corinthians 10:5)

The sword in the spiritual realm is God's
word. So, your sword is not in your hand. It
is in your mouth. (Ephesians 6:17)

God, the true God, will honor your decision not to
choose him as your God. (Deuteronomy 30:19)

Once a word is spoken it cannot be called
back, so choose your words carefully.

To change your world, you first
have to change your words.

Waiting patiently is a virtue.

Some people will try to destroy what
they want but can't have.

When God is number one in your life, no one else or nothing else can be number two, or number three, or number four, etc. Whatever you do, you do it as unto God, even if what you do is mundane or insignificant.

> Woe to those who have a crown of pride.
> Time will cause your glory and beauty to
> become a fading flower. (Isaiah 28:1)

> For your words to be believable, they must be
> confirmed by your actions. (Mark 16:20)

> Cause your life to be like a love letter written
> to your beloved. (2 Corinthians 3:2-3)

> A word of wisdom to preachers: Make your
> pulpit an alter and sacrifice your pride on it.

> Don't try to create an identity. Rather, receive
> your identity that God has selected for you.

A near death experience can give you an appreciation for life, the life that you now take for granted.

> God did not ask the Levites in the book of
> Leviticus to start the fire. God started the fire,
> which was symbolic of God's Holy Spirit, who

was made available to everyone when the New Testament was established. (Acts 2:3-4)

Emotional people are attracted to emotional people.

To reach God, go to 911. (Psalms 91:1)

If you sold your soul to Satan, what would you expect to receive in return? Do you believe Satan will supply what you expect? If he does, you can be assured that he will also supply you with some things that you don't want.

The peace that Jesus wants to give us is not like the peace the world tries to give us. (John 14:27)

If you have intimate relationships with Satan, you are apt to conceive and give birth to a strange child. (Hosea 5:1-7)

If you rejoice in the true God, he will restore the years of your life that the locust have eaten, or the caterpillar, or the canker worm, or the palmer worm. (Joel 2:23-25)

A foolish son is a grief to his father, and bitterness to his mother. (Proverbs 17:25)

Falling does not cause you to be a loser.
What causes you to be a loser is your refusal
to get back up after you have fallen.

Eat better to improve your life, not just so
you can have a better physical appearance.

Even if you can't sing, you can still make
God your song. (Isaiah 12:2)

Are you getting ready for your next life?
Noah didn't wait until it started raining
before he started building the Ark.

People demand their rights, but they never
demand their responsibilities. How long will we
have rights if we neglect our responsibilities?

A master deceiver will mix some truth with a lie in
order to make the lie believable. Watch for it.

Men who want to get married would be wise
if they ask God to select a wife for them. You
may be worried that God might select you a
wife that looks like a dump truck. Remember,
God looks on the heart, and so should you.

Don't limit God by your limited understanding
of him. (Psalms 78:37-41)

Blessed is the nation whose God is
the true God. (Psalms 33:12)

Be cautious about seeking fame. It
promises more than it delivers.

If you have faith only in yourself,
your world is too small.

How can you refrain from weeping when someone
you love deeply is eating food or following a life
style that you know will eventually ruin them?

Our outer worship of God cannot be a substitute
for our inner worship of God. (John 4:19-24)

How can we expect God to turn toward us if we
refuse to turn toward him. (Zechariah 1:8)

Learn from your past, but don't dwell on
it in your thinking. Think of your future.
There is no future in your past.

God will show himself toward those
who show mercy. (Psalms 18:25)

When you find yourself in darkness, ask God
to light your candle. (Psalms 18:28)

When you are angry, you think with
your emotions rather than your mind.
Emotions can be a wisdom killer.

God expects his servants to be overcomers,
overcome evil. We overcome evil with good.
(Romans 12:21; Revelation 3:5)

The Kingdom of God is not for sissies. The
Kingdom of God suffers violence, and the
violent take it by force. (Matthew 11:12)

How difficult would it be to think of
yourself as a friend of God?

If you don't like total darkness, you won't like
hell. Total darkness is a darkness you can feel.
(Exodus 10:21)

God's servants do not fast to get God's attention.
They already have his attention. They fast so
God can get their attention. (Isaiah 58:6-7)

As strange as it sounds, the conflicts you face in life
help mold your character, whether for good or bad.

If Satan and his followers are persecuting you, rejoice. You are a threat to Satan's kingdom.

The strength of your commitment toward God will determine the strength of your service toward God.

Religious church people run a risk of putting more emphasis on a holy place than they put on the Holy Spirit. (Acts 6:13)

Even if we meet God's conditions for going to heaven when we die, we can still live a defeated life here on earth if we don't ask God to help us with whatever is defeating us. (Matthew 7:7-8)

One of the reasons that people don't take seriously what happens after death is because they have no concept as to how long eternity is.

Our flesh does not like to wait. This is why we have difficulty waiting for God to answer our prayers.

Being a servant of God does not mean we will not die from persecution. But it does mean that our death will not be a hurtful experience. It will be like going to sleep, so much so that the bible even refers to the death of God's servants as "sleep". (Acts 7:60)

Don't even look at forbidden fruit. If it looks
good, it will create a desire in you. (Genesis 3:6)

In serving God, there is no substitute for obedience;
not even a large donation of money or property.

How can you have boldness when your life
ends and you know that the day of judgment
is at hand? (1 John 4:12, 17, 18)

You cannot run away from your personality
problems. Everywhere you go, there you are.

Some people's greatest fault is believing they
are faultless. All of their problems were
caused by someone else. (Genesis 3:13)

God allows us to judge people's
actions, but not their motives.

God may test you with something you don't like to see
if he can trust you to properly handle what you do like.

If your mouth gets you in trouble, there is
a good chance that your mouth can get you
out of trouble if you use it properly.

Jesus is the Prince of Peace. When he is in
your life, you will experience peace.
(Luke 2:14; Acts 3:15)

Men, if your girl friend is not your best
friend, you are not ready to get married.

Never give up what you know for what you
don't know, regardless of how good it looks.
Never trade a certainty for an uncertainty.

You cannot judge a book by its cover. You need to
read it before judging it. You cannot judge people by
what you see on the outside. Get to know their heart.

It would be wise not to be a companion with
anyone whose mouth is an open sepulcher, or
those who flatter with their lips. (Psalms 5:9)

If you are going to praise God, do it now. You
can't praise him from your grave. (Psalms 6:5)

Do not do anything dishonorable. It is not only on
you that dishonor descends, you can't hurt yourself
without hurting your friends. (Joshua 7:1)

King Solomon not only asked God for wisdom, he
also asked for knowledge. (2 Chronicles 1:11)

And he asked for understanding. (1 Kings 3:9)

Husbands, for a successful marriage,
don't just think of your wife as your wife.
Think of her as your bosom buddy.

The bible says Samson used the jaw bone of an
ass to kill 1,000 of his enemies. Is it probable
that some preachers have used the same weapon
to kill people's intimate relationship with a
good God? (Judges 15:15; Matthew 23:13)

After you have told God what is on your
heart, ask him what is on his heart.

Compassion for others will sometimes seem
like a burden, causing you to weep.
(Jeremiah 9:1-3)

In your prayer to God, include this in your
prayer, "Lord, in your wrath remember mercy."
(Habakkuk 3:2)

If the devil controls your mouth (words), he can
control you. And control what comes against you.

Don't walk according to your feelings,
walk according to what you believe.

If you want to demonstrate the Kingdom of God, first get to know the King of that Kingdom.

If you are going to teach anybody anything, the first thing have to do is to get their complete attention. Could this be the reason that Jesus mixed healing and teaching?

Some would consider it foolishness that God would have his only begotten son crucified. The foolishness of God is wiser than the wisdom of men. (1 Corinthians 1:25; Isaiah 53:4-5)

If we are oriented toward God, even our sighing becomes part of our prayer. (Mark 7:34)

Pride is not a good thing to have. It is listed in the bible with deceit, adultery, theft, etc. (Mark 7:20-23)

# 9

The Sabbath Day was made for man, not man for the Sabbath. (Mark 2:27)

God said, "Let there be light." And there was light. God saw what he said. We are made in his image. We see what we say, whether our words are good or bad. So, choose your words carefully. (Genesis 1:3; Proverbs 18:21)

It is not sufficient to just hear God's voice. We must be able to discern if the voice we are hearing is actually God's voice. Satan can mimic voices. Ask the voice if Jesus came to the earth in the flesh. If you don't get a reply in the affirmative, the voice you heard was not God's voice. (1 John 4:1-3)

If your tongue can be the pen of a ready writer, your pen can be the tongue of a ready speaker. (Psalms 45:1)

Notice what you say when you talk to yourself. It will reveal you to you.

When you are young, you will attend a lot of weddings. When you are old, you will attend a lot of funerals.

If you don't take charge of your thinking, someone else will. But you are the one that will bear the consequences of your thinking, whether good or bad.

God is a jealous God. He resents it when his betrothed goes a whoring after another god. (Exodus 34:14-17)

Being religious does not mean that you worship the true God. (John 8:44)

If the true God is your God, when you travel from life to death, God will do the driving. (Psalms 48:14)

A preacher's voice should be like a trumpet, calling us to battle in the spiritual realm. (1 Corinthians 14:8)

The entrance of God's word into our minds
brings light (spiritual light). Without God's
word, we pray in darkness (spiritual darkness).
(Psalms 119:105,130)

Some people are the most contented when
they have something to worry about. But
worry will descend into fear.

Trust God with your life. He will redeem
your life. The fear of death will no longer
have dominion over you. (Psalms 49:15)

The purpose of wealth should be to bless you, and
allow you to be a blessing to others. (Genesis 12:2)

The pleasures of sin will compete with
our joyful relationships with God.

If God's word is with you, God himself
is with you. (Joshua 1:8; John 1:1)

Those that are led by the Spirit of God are
the children of God. (Romans 8:14)

What do you do when wisdom comes against
your beliefs? Which one is apt to win? It will
depend upon your commitment to the truth.

God's word is truth, but we can't just base the truth on our favorite verses, include those that are not your favorite verses. (John 17:17)

A lazy man who does not want to go out and work will convince himself that there are lions in the street. (Proverbs 22:13)

Don't be concerned when dogs act like dogs. Be concerned when those who claim to be God's servants act like dogs.

God does not control the world's kingdoms. He gave Adam dominion. Satan deceived Adam and took over his dominion. (Luke 4:5-6)

However, the day will come when the last Adam (Jesus) will regain dominion. (1 Corinthians 15:45; Revelation 11:15)

Do you know any Christians who feel more comfortable with Jesus' cross than they do with Jesus? It is because Jesus' cross doesn't talk back.

When you get close to a person's pocket book, you are getting close to their heart.

The love of money is the root of all evil. If you want to find the source of evil, follow the money trail.

If God's word is with you, God is with you. (John 1:1)

Do you have a right to claim God's promises if you have refused his discipline? (Psalms 50:16-17)

God has promised us a 120-year life. But it is not automatic. We have to open our mouth and claim it, then live like someone would live who wants to live to be 120.

If the true God is the center of your life, life is good even when it is bad. That does not sound like wisdom, but it is. When you are with God, bad days don't seem so bad. Take notice that this applies only if God is the "center" of your life.

It can be disheartening to know there is a war going on between your spirit and your flesh. (Galatians 5:16-25)

Show God your face, not your back by walking away from his instructions. (Jeremiah 32:33)

God accepts our praise of him even when we don't feel like praising him. He views this type of praise as a sacrifice. (Jeremiah 33:11)

Don't tell God how much you love him if you refuse to forgive those who abuse you or despitefully use you, as God commanded you to do. (Matthew 5:44)

What does it benefit you if your words are smooth as butter, but war is in your heart? (Psalms 55:21)

The only time a married couple exchange vows is on their wedding day. For the rest of their marriage they are apt to exchange feelings without remembering their wedding vows.

You cannot be truly free until you know the truth about yourself.

Don't judge Christ by what Christians say and do. Rather, read the part of the bible that involves Christ himself.

God is a Spirit. Our bodies are made out of dirt. Dirt cannot worship God. We can only worship God through our spirit. Our spirit connects with God by our words. (Psalms 91:15; John 4:24; 6:63)

Don't be stressed over what you cannot change. Cast that care over on God, using words to do the casting. (1 Peter 5:7)

Hell is continuous night time, but no one can rest because of the pain. It goes on and on forever. Making plans not to go there would be an act of wisdom.

Whatever pleasure that is keeping you away from God now will be used to torment you in hell. You can be sure that God knows how to torment.

Confess your sins to God. He is the only one who can remove them from you as far as the east is from the west, and give you peace.

Don't just confess your sins to God to receive forgiveness, but also forgive yourself. When Satan tries to put you back on a guilt trip, hit him with Second Corinthians 10:5.

Ask God to fill your cup with his favors until your cup overflows. (Psalms 23:5)

We can receive God's promises only by our faith and patience. (Hebrews 5:12)

To receive the life that God talks about in Deuteronomy 30:19, we must use words. The same type of words that Jesus spoke during his earthly ministry. (John 6:63)

There is no such a thing as a free lunch. You may not have to pay for it, but somebody has to pay for it. Don't let anyone deceive you about this.

The ideas you have about yourself are more powerful than what others think about you.

We are the most like God when we give. God so loved the world that he gave. (John 3:16)

If you are fearful, know that your fear did not come from God. The fear that rebels have is a result of their rebellion against God. (2 Timothy 1;7)

If you seek the true God whole heartedly, you will find him. (Jeremiah 29:13)

God will sometimes purposely hide himself so that only those who are persistent will find him. So, be persistent. (Isaiah 45:15)

If you have committed yourself to God, you no longer belong to you. (1 Corinthians 6:19)

Is your mouth out of control? No? Are you sure?

A self righteous person is just as much in bondage
as a person who wants to commit suicide.

Compassion can sometimes be so strong that it feels
like a burden rather than a blessing. (1 Peter 3:8)

Would you look forward to your death if your
casket was made out of gold, or does gold
lose its value when you are facing death?

Don't just tell someone you love them,
show them that you love them.

Still your emotions and know that the true
God is truly God. (Psalms 46:10)

The lust of the eyes is just as powerful as
the lust of the flesh. (1 John 2:16)

Pleasing our flesh is not the same as
pleasing God. (Romans 8:8-10)

If you are a carrier of God's Spirit, you have
become peculiar, peculiar by the world's
standards. (Exodus 19:5; Titus 2:14)

Those who roar like a lion will mourn like a
dove if they don't prepare for Judgment Day.

Without God's Spirit residing in us, we cannot experience God's power and demonstrate the Kingdom of God. (Mark 16:20; Acts 1:8)

We don't connect with God by struggling. We connect with God by yielding, by surrendering. (Romans 6:19)

A wise person is one who can get out of a bad situation. But the wisest person is one who does not get in a bad situation in the first place.

Notice what it is that you focus on. What you focus will influence your life, whether for good or for bad.

Whatever we do for others as a servant of God, we should do it as if we are doing it for God. (Matthew 25:40)

Be cautious about building walls around yourself for protection. They may offer some protection, but they will become your prison.

Forgiving others is not keeping a score of wrongs. It is losing count. (Matthew 18:21-22)

If you are in bed with depression, you are in bed with a snake. Grab your bible and beat him over

the head by quoting the scriptures out loud.
(Mark 16:18; Luke 10:19; John 14:13-14)

God's wisdom is God's Spirit. Also known
as the Holy Spirit. (Isaiah 11:1-2)

Our fervor for God is determined by how
diligently we seek him. (Jeremiah 29:13)

Some church members may believe Jesus is
pleased with them if they do most things right.
How many husbands would be pleased if
their bride was faithful most of the time?

The more we are in tune with God and his Spirit,
the more patience we will have. (Romans 15:4)

Persistence is just as important for our involvement
with God as it is in our involvement with the world.

What is driving you? Who is driving you?
Who has the responsibility for driving you?

For God, timing is crucial. The bible says in the fulness
of time such and such happened. (Galatians 4:4-5)

Any preacher who preaches only comfortable religion has obviously not put on the mind of Christ. (Matthew 13:15; Philippians 2:5)

Your biggest enemy is fear, unless you believe God is with you all the time. (Deuteronomy 31:6; Hebrews 13:5)

If we ask, God's Spirit will help us love the unlovely. (Romans 5:5)

In order to be a child of God, we must be led by the Spirit of God. (Romans 8:14)

Pray for the salvation of your enemies. It is not only biblical to do this, it will energize your prayer time. (Luke 6:28)

Hear the wisdom of the writer of Psalms 62:8, "O my people, trust in God all the time. Pour out your heart to him. He is our refuge."

How high do you want to go in your relationship with God? Your attitude will determine your altitude. (1 Corinthians 6:17)

It is somewhat scary, but God knows what you are thinking. So be careful what you think. (Hebrews 4:12)

## Roy Martin

It is very difficult to be gracious to someone who believes they deserve it. No matter how much you do for them, it is never enough. They think you should have done more.

# 10

God's word is to your spirit what food is to your body. God's word nourishes your spirit.

God promises those who seek him with their whole heart will find him. (1 Chronicles 28:9)

If you don't accept the true God as your God, you will find yourself entering into darkness when you die. When this happens, speak these words: "Jesus, save me." Repeat this as many times as you need to. Will your words have a positive effect? I don't know, but it is worth a try.

When you realize that your death is imminent, don't be surprised to hear a voice say, "What did you do with your life?" It would be an act of wisdom on your part to ask yourself those words now.

Relationships are more important for a sense of fulfillment than your accomplishments in this world.

Would you believe that Jesus loves you more than you love yourself?

Your enemies may view you as a rug they can walk on, but God has obligated himself to protect you if you are his servant.

God's light shines continuously. Day and night are alike to God. (Psalms 139:12)

God can be trusted to never break his covenant with mankind, but mortal man is not as trustworthy. (Psalms 89:34, 118:8)

Words of wisdom from Moses to his people would apply to God's people today. (Deuteronomy 31:27)

Say to your soul, "Soul, be at rest and focus on God's promise to supply what I need." (Psalms 62:5; Philippians 4:19)

Bitter words are like arrows shot at those who are made in God's image. (Psalms 64:3; Genesis 1:26)

Hear the wisdom of God, "I know the thoughts
I think toward you. Thoughts of peace and
not evil, to give you a future and a hope."
(Jeremiah 29:11)

Take control of your mind, or else it will
become a battleground. As a man thinks in
his heart (mind) so is he. (Proverbs 23:7)

If you are busy nursing your grudges, you won't
smell the flowers or hear the birds singing.

There is a difference between a religious
spirit and God's Spirit. (James 1:26)

If you honor Jesus' cross more than you honor
Jesus' words, then the cross for you will be like the
golden calf that the Israelites honored when they
came out of Egypt. (Exodus 32:3-6; Isaiah 42:17)

The true test of true love is when you love those who
don't love you. Obviously, this type of love has to
be based on a commitment, rather than a feeling.

The way some people revere Jesus' cross,
it is obvious that they believe the cross
suffered and died for their sins.

Do you appreciate it when your spouse confesses your sins for you? You should appreciate it if you have not confessed them, and you don't want hell to become your eternal home. In marriage two become one, so they can confess each others sins if they do it for the right reason.

It is difficult to believe that your destiny is in your mouth, in your words. Both life and death are in the power of your tongue. (Proverbs 18:21)

It is comforting to know that when we do something that grieves God's heart he still loves us.

The most effective method for separating people from God is to keep them laughing. No one will confess their sins if you keep them laughing. You can be sure Satan knows this. Could this be the reason that the highest paid people on television are comedians? It is difficult to grasp that laughter can keep you from going to heaven. Preachers, don't be surprised if Satan tries to turn you into a comedian.

The most profound sin we can commit is not trusting God and his word. (1 Corinthians 1:9-10)

If God is a righteous judge, would he pronounce you NOT GUILTY? He will if you have confessed your sins. (1 John 1:9)

Preachers, if you don't preach the kingdom of God, you are not preaching the gospel, because the gospel is the gospel of the kingdom. (Matthew 24:14)

God's servants must be on guard not to develop an orphan mind set. God said he would never leave us nor forsake us. (Deuteronomy 31:6)

If we believe a lie, we will live a lie. This is what happened to Eve in the Garden of Eden. Ask God to help you interpret those words that are coming toward you every day.

You can't worship God, and worship yourself also. This is the same as worshipping two gods.

God's Spirit is God's presence. If you have God's Spirit in you, you have God's presence in you. (1 Thessalonians 2:19)

Depend of God to help you dream big dreams. Then depend on him to help you fulfill those big dreams.

Referring to God as your father brings joy to his heart. Jesus always referred to God as Father, except when he hung on the cross dying for sinners. Then he addressed God as God, which seems to imply that that there is no intimacy with God by sinners.

> Our faith in God is not just for the future. It has to be now, even though it involves the future. (Hebrews 11:1)

Don't spend all of your time serving yourself. Don't go down that street. It is a dead end street. (Acts 20:35).

> Jesus said those preparing for coming events are wise, surely this would include preparing for death. (Matthew 25:2,9)

According to the bible, in Jesus was life and his life was light. If we want to know more about that light, we need to study Jesus' life. (John 1:4)

God can make his voice sound like thunder. (Job 40:9) But he would prefer to talk to us as a friend would talk to a friend. (Exodus 33:11)

Fear is like a school yard bully. God did not
give us a spirit of fear. (2 Timothy 1:7)

Don't be ashamed of your scars. They are proof that
God heals, whether physically or emotionally.

When we have been comforted by God, we are in
a position to comfort others. (2 Corinthians 1:4)

Just because you enjoy sinning doesn't mean
you will enjoy the consequences of your sins.

If you want to clean up your life, you first have to
clean up your mouth, the words you speak. Your body
will go wherever your mouth takes it. (Proverbs 2:12)

It is difficult to explain God's love to others if we
have never experienced God's love ourselves.

You will know you are God's servant when
you love what God loves and hate what God
hates.(Proverbs 6:16-19; John 3:16)

Life is safer when two walk together. If
one falls in a pit, the other one can help
him out. (Ecclesiastes 4:9-10)
They will also be accountable to one another.

Jesus is what we would refer to as God's right hand man. (Romans 8:34)

God is not so forgetful that he will forget your labor of love toward him. (Hebrews 6:10)

With the help of God's Spirit we can love the unlovely. (Colossians 1:8)

Elderly men are not always wise because age by itself does not produce wisdom. (Job 32:9)

God's servants will receive a garment of praise for their spirit of heaviness. (Isaiah 61:3)

Man's glory is money. God's glory is miracles. Those fully committed to God can have both. (Philippians 4:19)

The law of Moses in the bible was never referred to as an everlasting covenant. Yet, many believe that it is. If it is why did God create a new covenant? (Hebrews 8:7)

Be the chosen of God in your thinking. You become what you think, and walk according to your thinking. (Isaiah 65:2)

Why do mole hills sometime become mountains in our lives? It is because we add more dirt to it by focusing on it and continuing to talk about it.

Don't spend a lot of time trying to figure out why a problem happened in your life, just attack it. Later you can analyze it to prevent it from happening again.

God's word is not just his word. His word is his life.(Philippians 2:12-16)

We can't live higher than our revelation. So, if you want to live on a higher level, increase the lever of your revelation. The best source of revelation is God's words. It was from the bible that a man became convinced that the world was round rather than flat. (Proverbs 8:27)

Although preaching and projects are an essential part of the church, the church will not be attractive to the whole world unless the church members love one another. (John 13:35)

You may not know God, but God knows you. (Psalms 103:14)

Without God's Spirit there would be no kingdom of God on the earth. (Romans 14:17)

You don't need a special type of feeling to
forgive someone. You forgive them by an act
of your will. In the hard cases, call on God
to help you. Then pray for God to bless the
person that wronged you. (Matthew 5:44)

Trust God to rain upon your desert
if you are his servant. Your desert will
blossom like a rose. (Isaiah 35:1)

We are all like models on the runway of life. Be very
selective of the life style that you choose to model.

Invite God's Spirit to be your comforter, your friend,
your buddy, your bosom buddy. (John 14:26)

The way to obtain more power from God is to be
more surrendered to God. (Luke 10:19, 12:13)

If you revel in people's compliments, you will
die on their criticisms. Take compliments lightly,
then your life will have more balance.

Do you just eat your favorite dessert, or do you make
love to it while you are eating it? Can God compete
successfully with your dessert for your devotion?

God has a lot to offer you. It grieves his heart when you ignore him or half heartedly accept him.

Good leaders begin as good followers. Even bold lions begin by following their elders.

When Jesus was on the cross, our cross was on his mind. (Matthew 16:24; Luke 23:34)

You pay your vows by being obedient to your vows. (Psalms 116:14)

Speaking words of thankfulness is a sacrifice if you don't feel like being thankful. (Psalms 116:17)

Preachers, preach as if you expect God to show up during your sermon. The bible says God inhabits the praises of his people. So, make praising God a part of your church services. God will be obligated to show up. Nothing compares to seeing God show up. (Psalms 23:3)

Get ready. Get ready. Get ready for your next life. Noah didn't wait until it started raining to start building the Ark.

We can't use our flesh's desires to satisfy our spirit's desires.

A mocker cannot expect to find
wisdom.(Proverbs 14:6)

The prudent depend on wisdom to gain understanding
as to why they do what they do. (Proverbs 14:8)

If you are God's servant, his Spirit dwells
in you. (1 Corinthians 3:16)

We will taste God's goodness when
we trust him. (Psalms 34:8)

If you want to see "good", don't allow your tongue
to speak evil or deceit. (Psalms 34:12-13)

If you want to test your wisdom, use your
wisdom to determine why it is so difficult for
married couples to forgive each other.

Whoever made time, made a lot of it; but your
portion of that time is very limited, so use it wisely.

One of the signs that God gives you that
confirms you are in his presence is rest,
which is akin to peace. (Exodus 33:14)

It is unfortunate that the English language has only
one word for the various types of love. This makes

it difficult to understand the New Testament, which was originally written in the Greek language. The word "love" in John 15:13 is not the same as "love" in John 15:17. The "love" in John 15:13 can only come from God to those who accept him as their God. The "love" in John 15:17 comes from our commitment to do something, or to treat someone in a certain manner, such as marriage vows. Neither of these two types of love are based on feelings, but most people believe they are, making these scriptures unbelievable and marriages fragile.

To qualify for eternal life in heaven is not complicated, but it does require you to believe that Jesus is who the bible says he is, and that he did what the bible says he did. Then you have to say you believe this whenever you are with others, this is called "testifying". (Matthew 4:4; John 5:39; 1John 2:24-25)

If you are not yet convinced of this, keep reading the first four books of the New Testament until you become convinced.

We can never be fully satisfied until we sleep (die) and wake up in God's presence. (Psalms 16:11)

This book, WORDS OF WISDOM, obviously does not contain everything you need to know concerning wisdom. The purpose of this book is to whet your appetite so you will hunger for more wisdom, and do your own research concerning wisdom. Start with the bible.

# Epilogue

This book includes God's wisdom and the world's wisdom, but the primary purpose for the book is to exalt God and his wisdom. In the course of writing this book, I heard these from God, "Your pen is your pulpit." So, I took very seriously what I wrote in this book.

I hope you take these WORDS OF WISDOM seriously also. My hope is that you will grab these words of wisdom and run with them.

The bible compares speaking words to sowing seeds.

In the parable of the sower in the bible, we are apt to focus on the type of ground mentioned, but notice the sower (Jesus) sowed good seed in all types of ground. So, our job as sowers is to sow seed in all types of ground. We cannot tell in advance which soil will respond to the seeds sown.

Remember, just because a person has ears does not mean he has ears that are willing to hear. But we have to assume everyone has a hearing ear, and continue to sow seeds.

The words of wisdom in this book are only a portion of the wisdom you will receive from reading the bible for yourself. I strongly urge you to set aside a minimum of thirty minutes of your day to read the bible. To do this, you will probably have to forsake one of your favorite TV shows, but it will be worth it. Try it for one month and then you will know if it is worth it.

If you are new at reading the bible, I suggest that you start with the book called JOHN. Then read the books of MATTHEW and MARK and LUKE. These four books cover the era of Jesus' ministry while he was on the earth.

Jesus is the grand subject of the NEW TESTAMENT portion of the bible, so concentrate your bible study primarily on the NEW TESTAMENT. However, wait on studying the book called REVELATION until you are well established in the other scriptures.

I have written a book that explains the book in the bible called REVELATION. The title of the book I wrote is THE BOOK OF REVELATION FROM ALPHA TO OMEGA. You should be able to find it wherever books are sold. If you don't find it on a shelf, ask them to order it for you.

www.ingramcontent.com/pod-product-compliance
Ingram Content Group UK Ltd.
Pitfield, Milton Keynes, MK11 3LW, UK
UKHW022209230426
12048UKWH00016BA/735